# PRAISE FOR *GOD'S GIVERS*

"*God's Givers* is an invaluable tool for every leader who is concerned with helping others make eternal investments. It is a must read for not only the business leader but also the wise pastor who seeks a biblical approach for developing the proper spirit of giving."

J. Denny Autrey, DMin, PhD
Dean and professor of pastoral ministries
J. Dalton Havard School for Theological
Studies

"Will Stevens writes and teaches to inspire new generations to share, give, invest, and sustain our Christian mark upon the world of *caritas*—charitable benevolence… Stevens presents a biblical model of how to do this, and how to do it well. Get this book into the hands of your children, your church deacons and your pastor, and every family member dear to you. You'll be paying forward a blessing certain to change the heart of every reader."

Scott Preissler, PhD, MEd., MS
Executive director of the National Center
for Stewardship & Generosity

"*God's Givers* is a wonderful book to help remind us that giving is faith at work. Will has retold these Old Testament stories in a fresh way that sheds new light on what it means to honor God as stewards of all that He gives us. May the Lord use this work to encourage, inspire and bless His people."

The Hon. Jane Norton
Former lt. governor of Colorado

"*God's Givers* is a tremendous asset in helping our donors to consider not just the results of their giving, but to focus more clearly and deeply on the "why" of their giving. It will help every one of us give generously and enjoy the utmost confidence in God's provision."

Joe Baker
CEO and founder, Save the Storks

"Every Christian business leader needs to continually be challenged on how they are using business and finances for Kingdom gain. This book has once again caused me to step back from my selfish motives, check my ego, and examine how to keep Christ as my #1 priority in business, finances, and life."

Paul Ten Haken
President, Click Rain

"It is a delight to find a resource we will want to share with the hundreds of families we serve each year through ministries around the country. God's Givers can help families chart a heart course through the noise... This book will help those on that journey to find ultimate joy and rest in Him."

Dave Keesling
Cofounder, PhilanthroCorp
author of A Journey: Life in Real Time

"It's not easy to give away hard earned money... This book will get you unstuck. The author will unveil the heart of God through the lens of intentional giving. When you see how significant the act of intentional giving is to our Creator, you will be compelled to take action!"

Darryl W. Lyons
Cofounder of PAX Financial Group and
author of Small Business Big Pressure:
A Faith-based Approach to Guide the
Ambitious Entrepreneur

"In God's Givers, Will Stevens has given us a book that is at the same time biblically astute, imaginative, and intensely practical."

Dr. John W. Taylor
Professor of New Testament
Gateway Seminary

"Will Stevens is a true 'expert' in the area of stewardship. By focusing on Old Testament role models, he ties together the work God did through all of the Old Testament and all the teachings of Jesus in the New Testament. A giving spirit is the foundation for true discipleship. This book lays the foundation for living a generous life."

Paul Damon
President, Family Capital Management;
Grand Rapids, MI

"*God's Givers* is a fantastic tool to present the biblical message that the way we think about our wealth begins with the truths revealed in the Bible. What better place to find a source of inspiration for giving than the Bible. Will has reached deep into the Old Testament to share the biblical foundations of giving and the faith that moves the people of God to generosity."

Eric Koeplin
Financial advisor; Denver, CO

"This book does a wonderful job reminding the reader of… [the] incredible biblical truth… revealed in the Old Testament. May all who read it be inspired to give from a heartfelt expression of gratitude for our Wonderful Savior!"

Dr. Johnathan W. Gray
President/CEO, Georgia Baptist
Foundation

"…*God's Givers* is a remarkable source of inspiration to all… who give generously… We see in the stories of the Bible that God invites us to give, expects us to give, and blesses those who give. I encourage every ministry to share this book with their entire community!"

John L. Pudaite
President, Bibles for the World

"…*God's Givers*… [is] a rare collision of theology, history, and worldly wisdom…"

Kelley J. Schubert
CPA/CFP, Schubert & Company Inc.

"[Stevens's] Old Testament examples 'come to life' on page after page and shed light on the realities of biblical stewardship. Read this book and be informed as well as inspired!"

Dr. Matthew McKellar
Associate professor of preaching,
School of Preaching Southwestern Baptist
Theological Seminary; Ft. Worth, Texas

"It will change your heart, your life, your legacy and most importantly, it will change [you], all for the better."

Richard A. Lavinski
CPA, managing partner, East 57 Street
Partners & serial entrepreneur

"In this helpful and illuminating book… [you will] be challenged and inspired to a life of greater worship through increased generosity."

Lance Gentry
Senior pastor, Austin Bluffs Evangelical
Free Church

"A gifted storyteller, Will Stevens shares with us seven inspirational… examples of devotion, sacrifice, and giving [that] will provide needed encouragement and instruction to all who partake of the wisdom that can be found."

Bob Korljan
CPA, pastor, and tax advisor

"[Your] family and your business will be blessed as you stand on and implement the biblical giving principles illustrated in *God's Givers*. It is a great reminder that His Word is true, back then, now, and forever."

Carolyn A. Thompson
Attorney at law and founder of
Thompson Law, PC

"Giving blesses in at least four directions; those who are empowered by the resources to accomplish their ministry, those who understand good news as their needs are met by the service provided, the giver who sees fruit from the gift in his own life and the lives of others impacted, and God is honored as the ultimate Provider. The 'investment' returns can be amazing."

Dale Brown
President of Petroleum Strategies, Inc.
and President of Moriah Resources, Inc.

"Using biblical stories and reflective questions, Will Stevens challenges Christians to examine worship through how we prioritize our giving. For leaders and role models of a world in crisis, this book skillfully challenges each reader to consider intentional, sacrificial giving choices for building "lasting legacies" for the Kingdom rather than here on earth."

**Kittie W. Watson**, Ph.D.
President and Founder, Innolect Inc.
and Former Chair Department of
Communication, Tulane University

"Will Stevens was a talented, hard-driving and highly successful businessman pursuing money and the good life when God got hold of him and turned him every way but loose. The Lord then took his natural business talents and experiences and gifted him supernaturally to teach the fundamentals of biblical giving as an act of worship in order to please, honor and serve the Lord. His wise counsel concerning finances is greatly needed in our highly materialistic society and even in the Church where many people are being taught to give in order to get."

**Dr. David R. Reagan**
Founder and Director,
Lamb & Lion Ministries

"Will invites us to join him on a generosity journey through the First Testament to gain God-honoring direction, take appropriate action, and enjoy abundant blessings. He creatively inspires our hearts to understand the deep faith-building joys of helping build the Kingdom. Read and reread as you find the deeper meaning of generosity."

**Jim Fisher**
President and Founder,
Trinity Financial Partners

# GOD'S
# GIVERS

SEVEN OLD TESTAMENT
STORIES OF FEARLESS GIVING

# GOD'S GIVERS

---

## WILL STEVENS

Throne Publishing Group
2329 N Career Ave #215
Sioux Falls, SD 57107
ThronePG.com

# TABLE OF CONTENTS

# FOREWORD

When my father, Doug Kiesewetter, and I founded the Christian Community Foundation, today known as WaterStone, it filled an important void in the Kingdom community. As we worked with Christian families around the country on estate, tax, and business planning issues, there was a critical need for a distinctively Christian foundation, a trusted resource that could give assurance to Christian givers that their lifelong giving would be implemented in keeping with their faith-based, God-honoring values and commitments. What began in 1980 as a solution for a finite number of Christian families has, by the grace of God, blossomed into a ministry that has blessed more than three thousand families and provided more than half a billion dollars of resources to four thousand ministries and nonprofits and has, more importantly, transformed countless lives for Christ around the world. We believe that our mission reflects the work of Jesus's ministry: bringing the good news to the poor, binding up the brokenhearted, giving sight to the blind, healing the sick, and comforting those who mourn.

At its core, WaterStone is a ministry that serves givers with technical and administrative expertise on giving viewed through a range of tax and wealth management issues. We're very good at telling the story of "how" to give more effectively and more intentionally—by multiplying our clients' giving impact and minimizing their taxes. One of the blessings of serving the Christian community of giving is seeing how what begins as a dialogue about tax and economic benefits invariably becomes a conversation about strengthening one's faith and creating a legacy of giving in a family. As people carefully think about the impact of being stewards of the businesses and the financial resources that God has entrusted to them, the Spirit prompts individuals to consider carefully what it means to be a good and faithful steward, to honor God through giving, and to transfer the importance of stewardship to future generations. That connection between faith and finance is the heartbeat of WaterStone.

This book is part of an effort to communicate to the Christian community the "why" of giving. The foundation for why we give lies in our relationship with the Lord. Believe it or not, we are not the first ones to recognize that when we give, we love our neighbor and honor God. Through giving we honor God by serving his people through the ministries that are doing the Lord's work every day. The Old Testament stories in this book lay out for us a framework for how our giving reflects our relationship with the Lord, demonstrates our love for God, and manifests our love for our neighbor. We hope that these stories of old about giving will inspire this generation and future generations to create new God-honoring stories of giving today.

**Doug Kiesewetter Jr.**
*WaterStone, Chairman of the Board*

# INTRODUCTION

If we read most of the current popular Christian literature on giving, we have to ask a basic question: Is it true that giving always revolves around money? When the primary lesson we draw from the Bible about giving is focused on its financial aspect, we miss the complete biblical model. The Bible teaches us far more about giving than how to make financial contributions. Giving carries layers of meaning beyond the scope of economics.

A popular view of biblical giving proposes to divide the Bible into two schools of giving: Old Testament and New Testament. In this binary approach, giving in the Old Testament was a compulsory act, an obligation under the Law. People gave because they had to. The New Testament is different because giving becomes an act of grace, where people give voluntarily. There is a fundamental problem in making such a dramatic distinction between Old and New Testament giving though: it ignores the role of the Spirit.

Throughout the Bible, whether in the Old or New Testament, biblical giving reflects a spiritual dimension. People in the Old Testament often gave not because they had to but because they had a willing heart. In the wilderness, the people of Israel "gave willingly" for the building of the tabernacle (Exod 35:5). In the New Testament, people also gave freely, as when a collection was taken to support the poor in Jerusalem (Acts 11:27-30). In both cases, giving was rooted in the same biblical truth: when we give it speaks not just of our wallet but of our spirit. Giving is a fundamental mark of our walk in the Spirit. It is both an internal and external practice.

My aim is to explore biblical giving, both through its scriptural principles and through actual biblical profiles in giving found in the Old Testament. Giving is not just about what we do on the outside. Giving is about what God does in us and through us on the inside. Biblical giving is all about the willing heart that God gives us and what we do with it.

Within this framework, we will walk through seven stories of giving from the Old Testament. Each story contains archetypal givers and antithetical givers—characters who faithfully worship God through expressions of generosity, and characters who deny God's blueprint for giving through idolatry and unbelief. Ultimately, we will find that God himself is the central character and the ultimate giver in each story. In this book I want to make three central claims about giving: 1) giving is worship, 2) giving expresses faith, and 3) giving fosters community. Within each section we will see how giving is central to God's purposes and plans for his people.

My hope is that this book will allow you to explore your own patterns of giving—individually and as a member of a church or family. Because "God loves a cheerful giver," I also pray this book will engender heart-level transformation in you as you interact with the Old Testament's robust theology of giving. May the Lord who gives us life, who gives us our every breath, who grants us the blessing of children, who gives us trials to shape our hearts, who gave his Son that we might believe and have eternal life, teach us to reflect his glory through our giving.

# PART ONE
# GIVING IS WORSHIP

# CHAPTER ONE

# FIRST THINGS FIRST

When we hear the story of Noah, we latch onto certain elements—the ark, the flood, the rainbow. But what is central to the story is God's relationship with his people. That relationship is carefully illustrated as Noah and his family leave the ark and, for their first act, gather in communal worship. The example of Noah can dramatically impact us today and help reshape our approach to worship, giving, and family.

Imagine you are a passenger on the ark, a member of Noah's family. For the last year you have been inside a colossal wooden boat that God had commissioned Noah to construct. God's purpose for this ark was for you and your family to have shelter from a tremendous, worldwide flood—a flood of God's judgment on mankind, whose hearts had become filled with wickedness and depravity. The Flood was God's means of cleansing his creation of evil. Among all men on earth, God chose Noah to form his remnant. You have been blessed to join Noah, and for the last 364 days, you've been in a state of awe, amazed that God would spare you from the torrential waters. You are not sure what life will look like after the Flood, but Noah exhorts you daily to trust that God will provide.

You wake one morning and hear the momentous news from Noah. *The waters have subsided! The ark has landed!* The ark sits completely still on dry land for the first time in a year. The feeling is surreal. It's a miracle! Rising and running to the ark's entrance, you see Noah opening the huge plank door, which God himself had shut nearly a year before. Bright, warm light pierces into the ark as the door falls and crashes onto dry ground. The whole world appears before you—it's remade, but somehow you sense the echoes of all the voices of those people who did not heed Noah's warning of God's coming wrath.

Noah beckons and leads you and the family out of the ark and onto the earth once again. Going on ahead, Noah begins to busy himself. What's he doing? Why is he gathering stones and piling them atop a large earthen mound? Noah is erecting an altar. With the help of Ham, Shem, and Japheth, he brings a selection of the clean animals and birds from the ark to the newly built altar. With the whole family gathered at the altar, you stand with your eyes lifted as Noah begins to sacrifice the animals as offerings to God.

How did Noah come to this position—a new man in a new world? The Bible tells us that the Lord was angry at the wickedness that had infested the world and he vowed to blot out man from the earth. But God in his mercy chose one man and his family to be saved from destruction and serve his purpose—the redemption of a people for his own glory. God did not scour the globe seeking a man worthy of salvation; there was none, and God knew it and said of man: "Every intention of the thoughts of his heart was only evil continually" (Gen 6:5). For his part, Noah did nothing to earn his position as the Lord's building contractor and captain of his ark. Noah's salvation and commission were based solely on the fact that he had "found favor in the eyes of the Lord" (Gen 6:8). Only after Noah had found favor with God was he called a righteous man (Gen 6:9). God chose Noah and invited him to participate in his plan of redemption. For decades, Noah faithfully executed his divine assignment, planning the ark, gathering materials, and performing the labor. As he worked, Noah acted as the Lord's prophet, relaying for 120 years God's edict of judgment on the world.

When Noah and his family finally disembarked from the ark, Noah began another construction project. He built an altar, the first mentioned in the Bible, and gathered his family to worship and make burnt offerings upon it. Significantly, Noah's first act in the new world was to offer gifts to the Lord. Noah's dramatic first act—giving—cannot be overemphasized. The conventional wisdom of the world might have told him to "get settled"—to secure his family first. Noah had a huge new task ahead of him. We must remember that, because of the Flood, all civilization had to start over once Noah landed. He and his family needed to find shelter, gather food and drinking water, and begin family planning. Noah, in essence, had become a new Adam. "And God blessed Noah and his sons and said to them, 'Be fruitful and multiply and fill the earth'" (Gen 9:1).

Even with much work to do and a family to care for, Noah's absolute first priority was God. His first act, one of giving to the Lord a sacrificial gift, had four essential meanings:

1. *Past deliverance:* Noah was giving thanks to God for his deliverance from the judgment on the earth.
2. *Present affirmation of God's continuing presence:* The animals on the altar were a sin offering. Despite his family's deliverance and Noah's right standing before God, Noah acknowledged through this sacrifice that they were still sinful men and women separated from a perfect, holy God.
3. *Future provision, protection, and promise:* God had brought them this far, and the sacrifice today of their food supply, these precious clean animals would not impede God from caring for them in the future.
4. *Noah's consecration as God's servant:* Noah's offering on the altar represented his dedication of his whole being to the Lord's service, his consecration as king and priest of the new world order.

Some might read this part of the story and think Noah's actions were irresponsible. *Why would you delay your ground breaking? Why sacrifice your food source? What about your responsiblity as head of your family?* Contrary to common wisdom, Noah's act of worship and sacrifice exemplifies not only his thankfulness for God's deliverance through the flood but also his trust in God's provision for the future—his future and that of his family. Noah understood that his life was not his own. He belonged entirely to God. The same was true for his family. As the patriarch of the "new" human race, Noah knew the Lord had set him apart to serve as God's king and priest in the new world order. He had already been God's prophet for more than a century! In this light, Noah's sacrifice embodied his holy consecration to the service of the Lord.

## First Things First

Noah's example of giving in the face of trials and in the midst of family issues reminds us that *true* giving involves risk and sacrifice. Indeed, the presenting of offerings to the Lord was more than merely a sacrifice of animals. Giving to the Lord came at a cost to him *and* to his family. This kind of sacrificial giving in a time of crisis is only possible when God gives us the grace that enables us to have faith in his power and provision. God had commanded Noah to take two pairs of unclean animals and seven pairs of clean animals onto the ark. Why two unclean? Why seven clean? That must mean more for Noah and his family to eat! No. The Lord provided clean animals for the gifts of sacrifice Noah would make on the altar of worship.

The gifts Noah offered on the altar were accepted in dramatic fashion by the Lord, who acknowledged them "as a pleasing aroma." Noah's gifts, representing his thanksgiving, repentance, and dedication, constituted a pure offering of faith and obedience. The animals were clean on the outside; Noah's heart was pure on the inside. Noah expressed his faith through his giving. He deliberately turned his attention to God and worshiped *before* taking care of his own vital affairs. Giving was his first priority in the new creation.

Noah's relationship with God was not one to be kept in the closet. It is significant that Noah's giving to the Lord was not done in isolation; his family witnessed and joined him in his outworking of trust, obedience, and sacrifice to God. He demonstrated his own faith and faithfulness *in full view of* his wife, his sons, and their wives. The lesson for us is that giving is an act we perform as part of a community of faith. Before the tabernacle formed the center of a worship system replete with a formal priesthood and prescribed sacrifices, God expected fathers to act as priests over their households, interceding before God for their families through prayer, offerings, and sacrifices. As the newly appointed priest of the new creation, Noah established and modeled a pattern of giving for his family. For Noah, as priest over his household, worship and giving to the Lord took top priority.

Noah's priestly duties of interceding and giving at the altar signaled to his sons how they too would one day be priests over their families. Their obligation as family heads was to prioritize God in their daily lives and lead their families in worship through sacrificial giving—in essence, to make the Lord first. Noah invited his family to *remember* what God had done for them—sovereignly electing Noah out of a fallen world; giving him a divine commission; providing him with the time and resources to build the ark; sheltering his family from the flood; bringing them safely to land; and inviting them to participate in God's promised plan to make a people for himself. Through collective worship and giving, Noah's family defined their identity as a family and a people belonging to the Lord.

As he worshiped, Noah modeled for all mankind how a faithful servant of the Lord lives and acts. Noah's entire walk of faith is living witness to the power of God in his life—as a man in the world, as a man called out of the world, and as a man made to serve God in a new world. Starting with his obedience to God in constructing the ark, Noah rejected his old life and the godless ways of the world. Now, this first building project in the new world, the altar, was dedicated entirely to the worship of God with no material benefit to himself or his family.

Noah's priority of faithful living through the giving of his time, talents, and treasure is a model of how we too should live: with a singular passion for joining ourselves and our resources to God's plans and purposes.

When we consider Noah with fresh eyes, it may be that the ark was not necessarily the center of Noah's story. In fact, *Noah* isn't even the center of this story—God is. It was God who, in his sovereignty, graciously elected Noah to be his righteous representative of mankind. It was God who demonstrated his perfect justice by judging and punishing the rebellious evil world through the Flood. It was God who chose to establish a new covenant with Noah, even though Noah too was a sinful member of fallen mankind. This theme of God's sovereignty runs throughout this book: it is God who is at the center of life—Noah's and ours. God is always the main character; as such we must always make him the "first thing" in our lives.

Noah's example of dedicated living and giving to God was not just for his sons' benefit; it speaks to us today. Through his building of the altar and his dedication to worship, Noah shows us that giving, inspired by a willing heart, a heart directed to the Lord, honors God. When we give, we too should give thanks for all the Lord has given and entrusted to us; acknowledge our own sinful nature and powerlessness beside an omnipotent, loving, and just God; ask for forgiveness; and dedicate our lives, our resources, and our families to his service. Giving is a tangible expression of a faithful heart that strives to make and keep God first.

Our society today is replete with pseudoaltars. Men build altars to sports, entertainment, sex, money, and power. The cultural idols we worship today—sports stars and Hollywood celebrities—each send out a Siren's song to entice us to stray from our focus on God. What's worse, we live in a world that glorifies the "self" over the "other." Noah's self-sacrificing example is important for us today because he reminds us that the first priority is not "I"—it's God. When we put ourselves before God, we, the creatures, declare ourselves of more worth than the Creator. That is idolatry—putting what we cherish ahead of God. Noah's lesson for us is that God must be our first priority. God commands his people to live with their eyes on him at all times—in good times and bad. God must be in focus in everything we do, and we live out that priority in worship, when we give thanks and dedicate our lives and our resources to serve God's purposes, not the world's or our own. Giving is an expression of our faith.

Do you find it difficult to make godly sacrifices that might cost you or those near to you? Sure—we all do! But Noah helps us *remember* that God has already provided for us. Noah reminds us that God's faithfulness declares that we strive to be obedient, follow his commands, and be conformed to his will. Through his grace, God grants us, his people, the gift of generous hearts and equips us with hands that desire to give—even when it seems like folly to the world.

## *For Further Reflection*

1. What about this story most resonated with you? How can it be applied in your own or your community's life?
2. What is the significance that Noah's first act upon disembarking from the ark was to worship God?
3. What was the risk Noah took in sacrificing from his family's food source? Have you ever worshiped in a way that put God above either your or your family's safety?
4. How did Noah model worship to his family?
5. How can you model worship to your family and community the way Noah did?

# CHAPTER TWO

# GIVING HONORS GOD

The story of Noah gives us profound insight into how God's covenant people give. As Noah adopts a pattern of proper worship, we (even millennia) later learn a number of biblical truths. First, God desires for his people to trust him. Second, our correct posture toward him should always be one of worship. And third, sacrificial giving is an essential part of how we worship. In this chapter I want to press further into the Old Testament paradigm and practice of giving. What if God not only desires our giving but expects it? And what if our modern ideas about giving are different than his? To explore these questions, let's turn back to another well-known story in Genesis—the story of Cain and Abel.

Now Adam knew Eve his wife, and she conceived and bore Cain, saying, "I have gotten a man with the help of the LORD." And again, she bore his brother Abel. Now Abel was a keeper of sheep, and Cain a worker of the ground. In the course of time Cain brought to the LORD an offering of the fruit of the ground, and Abel also brought of the firstborn of his flock and of their fat portions. And the LORD had regard for Abel and his offering, but for Cain and his offering he had no regard. So Cain was very angry, and his face fell. The LORD said to Cain, "Why are you angry, and why has your face fallen? If you do well, will you not be accepted? And if you do not do well, sin is crouching at the door. Its desire is for you, but you must rule over it." (Gen 4:1-7)

## God Expects Us to Give

The story of brothers Cain and Abel centers on an offering. In another sense, we could think of the story as centering on *giving*. At this point in the biblical record, Adam and Eve have been banished from the Garden of Eden because of their rebellion against God. Rather than obey God's commands and uphold his order, they make themselves the arbiters of right and wrong, and they eat the fruit. Sin has effectively entered the entire created world, and sin carries consequences. God has cursed the serpent, the man, the woman, and the land (Gen 3:14-19). By the time of Cain and Abel, the first generation, sacrifice is a formal part of life. But why? Why do Cain and Abel bring offerings to the Lord?

The tragic consequence of Adam and Eve's fall in the garden was that their sins separated them from God's presence. God—being perfect and holy—does not tolerate the presence of sin. Sin is a mark of rebellion, choosing to do things our way rather than God's way. Genesis tells us that God walked with Adam and Eve "in the cool of the day" before sin broke the beautiful relationship between him and humanity. When Adam and Eve first recognized they had transgressed God's law, they tried to hide from him; they realized they were naked and felt ashamed before him. They attempted to cover their sins and nakedness with leaves. But what did God do? He performed the first ever sacrifice and covered his sinful children with animal skins. "And the LORD God made for Adam and for his wife garments of skins and clothed them" (Gen 3:11). For God to cover their sins blood had to be shed through sacrifice. The author of Hebrews tells us "without the shedding of blood there is no forgiveness of sins" (Heb 9:22).

Cain and Abel knew that to approach God, to enter into relationship with their Creator, they had to present offerings to him. They needed to make sacrifices—give—to the Lord. Moreover, their approach reveals that there was not just an expectation but a blueprint for how one was to approach God.

Through the example of their parents, the brothers were well versed in how to approach God on *his* terms—though we quickly learn that Abel understood God's terms better than Cain did. Even before the narrative reaches the brothers' presentation of gifts, we learn something very important: God *expects* his people to give to him from the fruit of their labors. But perhaps just as important, we learn that God expects us to approach him *on his own terms*. In our day, we generally give only when it is convenient—when it won't truly cost us anything of value. We give what is surplus, that which is expendable. However, this story reveals that God orchestrates the *when, how, and what* of our giving. In fact, the way we give makes the difference between God's acceptance or rejection of our gifts.

The story traces a pattern for how we are to approach God. First, Cain and Abel brought their offerings "to the Lord," indicating that there was a particular place where gifts were to be presented. Second, they went to the place of offering *together*, indicating that giving was not just an individual practice but something done in community. The nature of the offerings also indicated that God expected giving from the brothers to come in a certain form—they should not come with empty hands. And the quality of what they brought was also set by God; they should not offer simply what they fancied to give. But the looming question remains: Why was Abel's offering accepted while Cain's was rejected?

## Abel Accepted, Cain Rejected

In grappling with this question, we must notice an important point: both Cain and Abel brought to God an offering that represented the fruit of their work. "Now Abel was a keeper of sheep, and Cain a worker of the ground" (Gen 4:2b). Part of God's command to humanity was that every person *work*—to care for and steward the earth over which he had given man dominion. This is simply God's order. When we work, we honor that order; when we refuse to work, we reject God's order. The brothers' offerings were evidence that they had been doing their appointed work and understood that the fruit of their labor belonged to God.

The interesting lesson here is that in God's order, there is an intimate connection between work and worship. God commissions man to work, and man is responsible for the results. In Genesis 2:15, we read, "The LORD God took the man and put him in the Garden of Eden to work it and take care of it." Because God's provision for man comes through man's work, work is the means through which we honor God. The way we celebrate God's provision for us is by trusting him to transform our labor. That celebration of God's power in us and provision for us is what worship is all about. We joyfully trust the Lord for the fruit of our work through our labor. That outward expression of joy and thanksgiving takes the form of giving. When we give the production of our hands to the Lord, we honor him and keep his order.

## The Result

The meaning behind this portion of the story is twofold. First, we see that God does care about *what* we give to him through worship. Abel was obedient and honored God by giving him the first and the best. Abel's offering cost him something. Cain merely brought *an* offering. Second, we learn that there is a heart-level dimension to our giving. By God's design, worship is a combination of the external and the internal. God accepted Abel's offering because Abel manifested trust in God's order. Like Noah, Abel put first things first. Cain, on the other hand, approached God with a gift of his labors, but one without the qualities of "first and best," presented with a begrudging, sullen, selfish heart—one that evidenced his underlying unbelief. His common fruit offering revealed the true condition of his ungrateful heart. When God rejected his offering, "Cain was very angry, and his face fell" (Gen 4:5b). Instead of looking up to God in obedience, trust, thanksgiving, dependence, and worship as Noah did, Cain looked away from the Lord and harbored anger in his heart. Cain's act is symbolic of the broken relationship between God and man—a rift that even animal sacrifices cannot permanently remedy.

Cain's fallen countenance suggests a defeated look and disturbed spirit, and as a result he is visibly and terribly upset. At that point, God offered some advice: "If you do well, will you not be accepted? And if you do not do well, sin is lurking at the door; its desire is for you, but you must master it" (Gen 4:7). In effect, God offered Cain grace and gave Cain the opportunity to make a better choice. Either he could look away from the Lord and continue in bitterness toward his brother or he could place his trust in the Lord and adopt a heart of obedience and generosity, beginning to give earnestly as an expression of his faith in the Lord.

## Approaching God

Like his improper approach to God, Cain's descent into sin and rebellion from God started at the heart level and moved outward through his actions. It began with a spiteful attitude toward God and escalated into drastic actions directed against his brother. "Cain spoke to Abel his brother. And when they were in the field, Cain rose up against his brother Abel and killed him" (Gen 4:8). Frustrated with his own failures and flawed relationship with the Lord, Cain decided to destroy his brother's fruitful relationship with God. And thus, in one act of taking, Cain broke the two greatest commandments—to love God and to love his neighbor.

| ABEL | CAIN |
|---|---|
| Obedient | Begrudging |
| Faithful | Unbelieving |
| Generous | Selfish |
| Sacrifice | Murder |

*Abel and Cain's attitudes in action*

Cain's failure to love his brother teaches us a valuable lesson: we cannot truly love anyone until we first love God. We cannot learn to love our neighbor until we fully understand that *God loves us.* God's love is not just a feeling or emotion. God teaches us about love in his words and through his works—he reveals what love is by what he does for us. His greatest sign of his love for us is through his giving. "For God so loved the world, that he gave his only son, that whoever believes in him should not perish but have eternal life" (John 3:16). God reveals his character to us so that we might imitate him and be closely conformed to his Son. Through our own relationship with God we learn how to love others. The way we express our love for our neighbor is a mirror of the way God loves us—sacrificially.

The New Testament echoes the need to express our love. Jesus told his disciples, "If you keep my commandments, you will abide in my love, just as I have kept my Father's commandments and abide in his love. ... This is my commandment, that you love one another as I have loved you" (John 15:10, 12). Jesus commands us, as Christians today, to love one another, and he also models what that looks like.

One way we love our neighbor is through giving—we give our time, we offer prayers, we lend help in time of need, etc. Every opportunity to give is a test of our hearts. How will you respond to opportunities to give? Like Abel or like Cain? Does the thought of costly sacrifices make you cringe? It might. If we want our own hearts to be generous, it's a tremendous help to remember (like Noah at the altar) what God has graciously given us and done for us. In his second letter to the church at Corinth, Paul urges this kind of remembrance: "For you know the grace of our Lord Jesus Christ, that though he was rich, yet for your sake he became poor, so that you by his poverty might become rich" (2 Cor 8:9). When our hearts melt at the thought of God's sacrificial love for us, we will be able to give as Abel gave—with obedience and joy—even when it costs us greatly. But if we forget or ignore what God has done for us, we will quickly be overtaken by our own selfish worries and wants, like Cain.

Have you passed the tests of giving that God has placed on your path? Do you seek ways to love your neighbor through generous, even costly giving? If we're honest, we'll confess to feeling a closer identification with Cain than with Abel. God expects us, his people, to give. We can be secure in the knowledge that our loving Father has already provided us with everything we need: money, time, relationships—they all come from and belong to God. God is inviting us to give and to live on his terms, not our own. We will continue to flesh out what this type of stewardship living looks like through the rest of this book. For now, as we remember God's love for us in Jesus, we each must face his fateful words to Cain: *If you do well, will you not be accepted?*

Giving expresses our walk with the Lord. It is a way for us to gauge the deepest desires of our hearts, either in alignment with God's ways or with our own. Cain and Abel gave in very different ways, externally and internally, and those differences revealed the contrast between a man of faith and a man of unbelief. Hebrews 11:14 comments on Abel's sacrifice as follows: "By faith Abel offered to God a more acceptable sacrifice than Cain, through which he was commended as righteous, God commending him by accepting his gifts. And through his faith, though he died, he still speaks." Through their giving, Cain and Abel revealed two very different hearts. One was that of a righteous man of faith; the other was that of a wicked man of unbelief.

## For Further Reflection

1. What about this story most resonated with you? How can it be applied in your own or your community's life?
2. Why was Abel's gift accepted while Cain's was rejected?
3. Does God expect us to approach him in worship and giving according to his terms, or ours? What are his terms?
4. In what ways has God modeled selfless giving for his people?
5. Examine your giving in the past year. What heart is revealed: one of faith, or one of unbelief?

# CHAPTER THREE

# A TALE OF TWO COLLECTIONS

The story of Noah reminds us how important it is to keep the first things first. When we prioritize God over our own needs, he promises to meet our needs. Cain and Abel remind us that God expects his people to give and worship in particular ways—externally and internally. Our obedience should mirror Abel's and spur our hearts to trust in the Lord's provision. Now I want to take a closer look at exactly *what* God expects us to give—and how he provides for those who trust in him. Turn with me to the book of Exodus. We'll pick up in chapter 35 as Israel is in flight from Egypt and heading into the wilderness, led by Moses.

## A Collection for the Tabernacle

Though the tabernacle collection took place after the infamous golden calf incident—which we will explore later this chapter—we will begin with this story of Moses's commission to build a dwelling place, a tabernacle, for the Lord and the people's participation through generosity. After four hundred years of brutal slavery and exploitative physical labor in Egypt, Israel was finally free from bondage. Though God seemed absent from his people for so long, he came through in miraculous ways—raising up Moses to lead Israel, raining down plagues on Egypt to show his power, and ultimately changing the heart of Pharaoh to let Israel go. God fulfilled his promise: "I will take you to be my people, and I will be your God, and you shall know that I am the LORD your God, who has brought you out from under the burdens of the Egyptians" (Exod 6:7). Before Israel embarked on a new journey, God gave his people a departure gift: the plunder of Egypt. God empowered the Israelites to take jewelry, gold, silver, and clothing from the Egyptians and carry it all into the wilderness (Exod 12:35-36). We'll return to this important point momentarily. For now, let's move ahead to the camp at Mount Sinai.

Like Cain and Abel, *all* of Israel suffered a broken relationship with God because of the sins of their first parents, Adam and Eve. But they also suffered because of their own sins. However, God was not content with this broken relationship. His desire was to dwell with his people. So, once Israel had left Egypt far behind them, the Lord gave Moses instructions to build a portable place where he would dwell with his people again—the tabernacle. In his instructions, God provided Moses with the detailed specifications for how the tabernacle was to be built (see Exodus 26), including exact dimensions, fabrics, types of wood, etc. But the overarching significance of the tabernacle was clear to Israel: *God wants to be with us!*

## Silver and Gold

How were the Israelites supposed to create a finely designed portable structure in the middle of the wilderness? Where will they find the right supplies? Here we must recall God's previous permission for Israel to take plunder from Egypt before the exile. Because of this Egyptian tribute, the people of Israel had enough gold, silver, and other materials to construct the tabernacle exactly as God instructed them. All they had to do was give it and build with it.

> The LORD said to Moses, "Speak to the people of Israel, that they take for me a contribution. From every man whose heart moves him you shall receive the contribution for me. And this is the contribution that you shall receive from them: gold, silver, and bronze, blue and purple and scarlet yarns and fine twined linen, goats' hair, tanned rams' skins, goatskins, acacia wood, oil for the lamps, spices for the anointing oil and for the fragrant incense, onyx stones, and stones for setting, for the ephod and for the breastpiece. And let them make me a sanctuary, that I may dwell in their midst. Exactly as I show you concerning the pattern of the tabernacle, and of all its furniture, so you shall make it." (Exod 25:9)

We see now that God's provision for Israel through the people of Egypt gave them precisely what they needed to build the tabernacle in the wilderness. Before they even knew where they were headed or what the plunder was for, God provided. Now, by God's plan, Moses was to take a collection from the people. This collection was an invitation from God for the people to participate in the experience of building a sanctuary for the Lord. Israel was being invited to create a dwelling place for God on earth through their God-given time, talents, and treasures. This chance to give was yet another opportunity for their commitment to faith in God. God had provided what they needed for the tabernacle project; now they were called to respond, to trust him and *give* back, rather than seeking out and securing their own safety.

God's invitation to contribute was extended to "every man whose heart moves him." This small verse is significant. It indicates once again that God looks not only at externals but at the heart of those who give to him. God only desires heart-driven generosity—giving that resembles Abel's joyful offering of his best, not Cain's reluctant, grumbling gift. Further, the story indicates that this was an opportunity for those with willing hearts to contribute to the project through their talents. (Not just anyone can build a tabernacle!) Exodus speaks of two particularly gifted men, Oholiab and Bezalel, who were commissioned and equipped by the Lord to lead the building process:

> The LORD said to Moses, "See, I have called by name Bezalel the son of Uri, son of Hur, of the tribe of Judah, and I have filled him with the Spirit of God, with ability and intelligence, with knowledge and all craftsmanship, to devise artistic designs, to work in gold, silver, and bronze, in cutting stones for setting, and in carving wood, to work in every craft. And behold, I have appointed with him Oholiab, the son of Ahisamach, of the tribe of Dan. And I have given to all able men ability, that they may make all that I have commanded you." (Exod 31:1-6)

In other words, God *blessed* Israel abundantly, not just with treasure, but with the skills and resources necessary to do his will, to create a place for him to dwell among them. He even filled workers with the specialized gifting of his Spirit! This coming together of God's Spirit with men's hearts is a critical place for us to pause and ask ourselves a few relevant questions: What resources do I have in my possession (more than just money) that I could give? What skills has God given me through which I could bless others? Do I consider my resources and skills as gifts from God to use for his purposes? These questions can be difficult to answer honestly, but before we can give our "first and our best" to the Lord, we must see what he has first given us, how he has equipped us to help build his Kingdom on this earth.

## A Collection for the Golden Calf

Unfortunately, the Israelites were not always resolute in turning their hearts and hands to the Lord. They had made a solemn promise as a nation to obey the Lord: "All the people answered together and said, 'All that the Lord has spoken we will do.'" Nevertheless, they strayed and committed a grievous sin. That betrayal of their pledge, that error in judgment, was the building of the golden calf. When Israel came to Mount Sinai, the Lord called Moses to meet with him at the top of the mountain. During the days Moses remained with God on the mountain, the Israelites grew impatient down below. The story unfolds painfully:

> When the people saw that Moses delayed to come down from the mountain, the people gathered themselves together to Aaron and said to him, "Up, make us gods who shall go before us. As for this

Moses, the man who brought us up out of the land of Egypt, we do not know what has become of him." So Aaron said to them, "Take off the rings of gold that are in the ears of your wives, your sons, and your daughters, and bring them to me." So all the people took off the rings of gold that were in their ears and brought them to Aaron. And he received the gold from their hand and fashioned it with a graving tool and made a golden calf. And they said, "These are your gods, O Israel, who brought you up out of the land of Egypt!" (Exod 32:1-4)

Though much could be said about this incident of idolatry, I want to focus on the collection from the people to create the golden calf. This collection stands in stark contrast with the collection Moses would later take for the tabernacle. The tabernacle was the place where God would dwell with Israel; but here we see Israel *giving* the gold and silver that God provided them not for the dwelling place for the Lord, but to create a god of their own—one they could touch and see. Israel committed the gifts God had provided, not to honor the Lord God, who had delivered them from Egypt, but to their own distorted desires. In an act that was nothing less than idolatry, they made a god in their own image, a god of their own imagination. They had forgotten that it was the Lord who had given them the gold and silver. They had forgotten it was the Lord who had truly brought them out of bondage in the land of Egypt. They forgot it was the Lord who had promised to dwell among them.

When Moses returned from the mountaintop, he was outraged at the people's idolatrous folly. In his fury, he melted down the golden calf, ground it to a powder, scattered it over the water, and made the people drink it. In essence, he made them choke on their own idola-try. Moses then commandeered a number of volunteers, men of the tribe of Levi, to run through the camp and kill any of those who had abandoned the Lord. "And that day about three thousand men of the people fell" (Exod 32:28b). Israel's misuse of God's resources (an act of idolatry) carried grave penalties. Rather than giving the Lord's gold and silver to God for his purposes, the people dedicated them instead to the fabrication of a false god. The evil work of their hands revealed forgetful minds and ungrateful hearts. They forgot that the Lord's desire, plan, and promise was to make a people for himself and to be with them (Exod 32:13). In their willful forgetfulness, they replaced the Living God of Abraham, Isaac, and Jacob with one that they created from the very gifts he had given them in Egypt. They gave willingly to a god of their own folly.

This "tale of two collections" presents us with a dichotomy of biblical giving. The first collection we examined was an invita-tion by God for "every man whose heart moves him" to give time, talents, and treasures toward building the tabernacle and participate in God's plans; it was an opportunity to express their faith through *giving*. The second collection was for a plan hatched in the minds of wicked men—the construction of the golden calf. What lessons can we learn from these collections?

God still seeks generous-hearted worship from his people. He still calls his children to steward their time, talents, and treasures in ways that honor him and build his Kingdom on earth. But before we join ourselves to God's work, we must acknowledge that all of our "gold" is a gift from God; everything we have to offer *to* him is only a gift *from* him. As David said, "LORD our God, all this abundance that we have provided for building you a temple for your Holy Name comes from your hand, and all of it belongs to you" (1 Chr 29:16). God does not need us, his people, to provide for him. Rather, as Christians we understand that God has invited us to participate in his plans according to his purposes—to help build his dwelling place, as it were. We have the unique joy of offering our resources to churches, ministries that do the work of the Lord. Through our giving we glorify God and serve our neighbor. Fearless giving might be difficult for you—perhaps you don't have much financial margin from which to give. But as we decipher what and how God might have us give, we must begin by remembering that God has already graciously provided everything we need. He's even provided us with the very gifts—time, talent, and treasure—that we are to give back to him!

Further, we should draw our attention to the communal nature of giving pictured in the tabernacle narrative. God invited *anyone* with a willing heart to come together as a people of faith and give. The community was to pool their resources together so that their work might be as effective and fruitful as possible. Like all spiritual disciplines, giving is something that is meant to be done in community with other brothers and sisters in the Lord. Do you belong to a community of givers? Does your church regularly dispense its resources to help build disciples and spread the gospel?

I hope this chapter stirs you to begin a sort of spiritual audit of your heart's commitment to giving—as well as the "heart" of your church. God's desire and expectation is that his children give generously to him by serving each other, trusting in him to meet their needs. This spirit of community and communal giving is a mark of the true church. We are collectively the One Body of Christ, and through giving each of us grows more Christlike. On the cross, Jesus embodied what fearless, heartfelt giving looks like. He simply calls us to trust and follow him with our own giving. "If you then, who are evil, know how to give good gifts to your children, how much more will your Father who is in heaven give good things to those who ask him!" (Matt 7:11).

## *For Further Reflection*

1. What about this story most resonated with you? How can it be applied in your own or your community's life?
2. In what areas has God already provided for the giving he is inviting you into?
3. What are the similarities between the tabernacle collection and the golden calf collection? What are the differences between the two?
4. Where have you committed the resources God has provided to you for your idolatrous purposes rather than his?
5. Where can you recommit the resources he has provided to you for his purposes, in time, talent, and treasure?

# PART TWO
# GIVING EXPRESSES FAITH

# CHAPTER FOUR

# CALLED TO BE GOD'S STEWARDS

So far in this book I have looked exclusively at familiar Old Testament stories. These texts are basically ubiquitous—taught in graduate-level seminars and in children's Sunday School classes. However, I now want to turn to a less celebrated chapter of the Old Testament's teaching on giving: the story of Naboth's vineyard in 1 Kings 21. I imagine some of you have never read this text or heard Naboth's name before. But this short text has a number of important lessons to teach us about giving. In fact, I do not believe we can afford to look past this story as we strive to become people who give like God.

## Naboth's Vineyard

One day the wicked king Ahab gazed out of his window at his neighbor's land. Naboth, his neighbor, had a fine vineyard that the king envied in his heart. After some deliberation, Ahab made up his mind: he had to have that vineyard. He paid a visit to Naboth and offered him a fair price in terms of either money or another piece of land in exchange for the vineyard—whichever Naboth preferred. But Naboth responded to the king: "The Lord forbid that I should give you the inheritance of my fathers" (1 Kgs 21:3). Naboth outright refused the king's offer because he implied it simply wasn't his to sell (Lev 25:23).

Ahab went home and sulked. Queen Jezebel, his devious wife, confronted him about his gloomy mood. When Ahab told her how disappointed he was not to have Naboth's vineyard, Jezebel took matters into her own hands. She paid off witnesses, concocted a few trumped-up charges against Naboth, and had him executed by stoning. "And as soon as Ahab heard that Naboth was dead, Ahab arose to go down to the vineyard of Naboth the Jezreelite, to take possession of it" (1 Kgs 21:16). Past the books of Kings, the Bible never again mentions poor Naboth.

It is easy to recognize the evil of Ahab and Jezebel. But what do we make of Naboth? What drove him to defy the king? Why not give the king what he wanted?

The simple answer is that Naboth was a man of faith and he refused to compromise his covenant obligations to the Lord. Naboth's covenant position was that of a steward. God had ordained that the land be apportioned among the tribes of Israel and subdivided along family lines forever (Num 34:13; Josh 13:7). That land plan was God's way of declaring ownership while allowing his chosen people to live fruitfully as caretakers of the Lord's allotted portion. It was Naboth's covenant duty to honor the Lord by guarding the vineyard and to use it as God had intended. Naboth reminds Ahab of God's gift of the land by referring to "the inheritance of his fathers." God had given the vineyard to Naboth's ancestors. It was Naboth's covenant duty to honor the Lord by guarding that gift, i.e., to use it in the manner God had intended.

The use of language in this story is compelling. Notice all the first-person pronouns Ahab used when he first asked Naboth for the land: "Give *me* your vineyard, that *I* may have it for a vegetable garden, because it is near *my* house, and *I* will give you a better vineyard for it" (1 Kgs 21:2, emphasis added). Now, King Ahab has not gone down in history as a particularly charitable figure. His moral character, his marriage to a foreign woman, even his entire reign as king over Israel were corrupt to the core. This brief instance manifested the self-serving gravitational pull at the center of his being. Rather than acknowledging God's blueprint for the land, Ahab "lay down on his bed and turned away his face and would eat no food" (1 Kgs 21:4b). Ahab was clearly no model citizen—even as king.

## Naboth's Refusal

When Jezebel asked her husband about the incident, he misquoted Naboth: And he said to her, "Because I spoke to Naboth the Jezreelite and said to him, 'Give me your vineyard for money, or else, if it please you, I will give you another vineyard for it.' And he answered, 'I will not give you my vineyard'" (1 Kgs 21:6). Did Naboth really say "*I will not give you my vineyard?*" No. Though this was likely how the king interpreted Naboth's words, what he really said was far more compelling: "The LORD forbid that I should give you the inheritance of my fathers" (1 Kgs 21:3). In contrast with Ahab's first-person pronouns, Naboth claimed the covenant name of the Lord (LORD in all caps represents YHWH, the covenant name God used to identify himself to Moses at the burning bush) as he explained why he could not give up the vineyard. Naboth's refusal to abandon his inheritance made his message to Ahab crystal clear:

1. The vineyard and all I have belong to the Lord.
2. God gave this land to my tribe, to my forefathers, and to me, and I am called to steward it for God's purposes.
3. No power on earth—no king or human authority—can overturn God's ordained order.
4. Stewarding the Lord's gifts is an expression of unbreakable faith.
5. Your desire to confiscate the property of the Lord is an act of sin, rebellion, and idolatry.

We can imagine any number of alternative responses Naboth *could* have given the king. "No thanks, Ahab. This is my vineyard. I will use it for my own grapes." Or, "Sure, Ahab, I'll take your money. You take the vineyard." But his actual response was God-honoring and filled with risk—demonstrating his deep-seated theological convictions about God's covenant with his people. Naboth never claimed to have personal title to the land; he simply acknowledged that God had given the land to his fathers. He actually confessed that he had no right to give it away, even to the king! His responsibility was to care for it himself on behalf of the true owner, the LORD.

By thinking that Naboth owned the vineyard, Ahab was guilty of a case of mistaken identity.

Naboth's obedience stands as a challenge to each of us. Put in a similar situation, would we choose to honor God rather than capitulate to a king? While you may never come face to face with the leader of your country, you do face Naboth-like choices every day—choices to bend to the rulers of the world or honor God's order. Christians, by nature, belong to the Kingdom of God. This Kingdom is radically distinct from the world. Jesus told us, "My kingdom is not of this world. If my kingdom were of this world, my servants would have been fighting, that I might not be delivered over to the Jews. But my kingdom is not from the world" (John 18:36).

## Naboth's Sacrifice

In terms of giving, this story presents us with two polar examples. On the one hand is King Ahab and Jezebel: without the slightest care for God, they grabbed for everything they wanted—no matter the cost. And the cost grew higher and higher as their conspiracy of sin sunk lower and lower. First Ahab *coveted* Naboth's land. Then he *lied* to Jezebel about Naboth's words; then she conspired with her agents against Naboth. Finally, she had him *killed*—stoned by her stooges on trumped-up charges. These two royals are an embodiment of a host of sins: idolatry, unbelief, hatred against God and his people, conspiracy against his people, lying about God's people, and ultimately murderous violence against them.

On the other hand, we have Naboth. In his faithfulness to God, Naboth suffered at the hands of the wicked Ahab and Jezebel. Because he chose to guard God's order, he was victimized, falsely accused, and murdered. As he defended what God had given him, Naboth was forced to pay the ultimate price, the cost of his very life. Through his rejection of God's order, Ahab declared himself to be the ultimate authority; through his faithfulness to God, Naboth declared God to be the ultimate authority—even under threat of death. Thus, by his defiant actions and sacrifice, Naboth declared that both the vineyard and his very life belonged to the Lord. Naboth embodied what Paul calls *spiritual worship* in Romans 12: "I appeal to you therefore, brothers, by the mercies of God, to present your bodies as a living sacrifice, holy and acceptable to God, which is your spiritual worship. Do not be conformed to this world, but be transformed by the renewal of your mind, that by testing you may discern what is the will of God, what is good and acceptable and perfect" (Rom 12:1-2).

## Naboth's Story

But where is justice in this story? Does God simply let Ahab and his malicious wife get away with their evil? No, he does not. As the narrative unfolds, we read that they both receive their just punishment, death, in a matter of time—Ahab in battle, while Jezebel is thrown from a tower and eaten by dogs. Nevertheless, Naboth remains dead. We must learn that choosing to steward what God has given us might actually cost us more than we could ever imagine. It might cost us everything—but God will bring his justice to bear, on his terms, in his time.

Though this story is less known than the other Old Testament texts we have looked at, Naboth's life prefigures Jesus's life in many compelling ways.

1. Naboth had a vineyard; Jesus is the true vine.
2. Naboth did God's will and did not bend to the temptations of the evil world, just like Jesus.
3. Both were paraded before kangaroo courts.
4. Both were accused by paid witnesses.
5. Both were convicted of the same crimes, blasphemy, and treason.
6. Both were executed outside of the city.

These resemblances to Christ remind us that Naboth is an archetypal figure for how we are to steward what God has given us. He helps us recognize that we are stewards not only of material possessions but of spiritual treasure. When we consider our possessions, do we focus on the fact that what we have comes from God and belongs to him? Or are we convinced that *we* own our cars, homes, finances, etc.? Do we carefully consider our obligation to be good and faithful stewards of all that the Lord entrusts to us?

Because Christians have the indwelling presence of God's Spirit in them, they *can* become people who give like God. Like Naboth, let our faith speak through our attitudes about our wealth and echo in our willingness and our joy to dedicate what we have to the Lord and direct it to his works, his ministries. Let us guard what the Lord has given us and glorify him through our spirit of generosity.

## *For Further Reflection*

1. What about this story most resonated with you? How can it be applied in your own or your community's life?
2. How did Naboth view the property he had inherited? Is this the common way our culture views inheritance?
3. How did King Ahab and Queen Jezebel view Naboth's vineyard?
4. In what ways did Naboth prefigure Jesus?
5. Where have you capitulated to the cultural view of property and resources rather than respected God's order and ownership?

# CHAPTER FIVE

# A WILLING HEART

Have you ever experienced abundant generosity? That is, have you ever been the recipient of someone's giving that was so overwhelming, so lavish, that you could never forget it? If you have, you understand how profound an experience this can be—when someone goes out of their way to meet your needs. If you have not, pay close attention to this chapter. Because now we turn to the Old Testament story of a man named Boaz—a man of valor and a radical, godly giver.

## A Man of Valor

Boaz is a central figure in the book of Ruth. The book begins by telling of a severe famine that had spread across the kingdom of Judah and hit the town of Bethlehem. We are first introduced to Naomi, who with her husband, Elimelech, decide to flee the famine, taking their two sons and leaving Bethlehem—the "house of bread"—for the foreign land of Moab. During this period, the time of the Judges, Israel was without a king. It was a dark time for God's people, during which "everyone did [what] was right in his own eyes" (Judg 21:25). Yet God had not abandoned his covenant with his people. After ten years in Moab, Naomi suffered tremendous losses. Her husband and then both her sons died. Naomi was left with her two Moabitess daughters-in-law. The fate of widowed women without male providers was not a promising one in those days. Despite Naomi's dramatic reversal of fortune and disadvantaged social status, Ruth committed herself to caring for her mother-in-law. Ruth gave her whole being—her future, and her life—to Naomi: "Where you go I will go, and where you lodge I will lodge. Your people shall be my people, and your God my God. Where you die I will die, and there will I be buried. May the Lord do so to me and more also if anything but death parts me from you" (Ruth 1:16-17). Ruth would accompany Naomi back to Bethlehem. Ruth's gift of loyalty was an act of faith in the God of Naomi. However, Ruth had her own issues. Ruth was also a vulnerable widow and a Moabitess, a foreigner in the eyes of the people of Bethlehem. To put it plainly, Ruth and Noami were two desperate women in a threatening, hostile world.

One day Ruth went to gather free food by going to glean in the fields of Bethlehem, where she and Naomi had settled. She happened to come upon the property belonging to Boaz, who, it turned out, was a near relative to Naomi's deceased husband, Elimelech. The foreman over Boaz's fields allowed Ruth to glean and gather grain, in accordance with the Law that required farmers to leave the edges of their fields unharvested so the poor, the needy, and sojourners could scoop up the scraps and feed themselves.

When Boaz appeared in the fields and greeted his workers, he distinguished himself as a man of God in his words and in his deeds. "And behold, Boaz came from Bethlehem. And he said to the reapers, 'The LORD be with you!' And they answered, 'The LORD bless you!'" (Ruth 2:4). Clearly he was a model employer, but the most prominent feature of his godly character was revealed in his giving. Like other Old Testament figures we have surveyed in this book, Boaz presents us with a model of what biblical giving looks like. Boaz was a man of courage, well-respected as a prominent citizen of Bethlehem. In action, Boaz's spirit of generosity exceeded the formal requirements of the Law to provide for the poor, the widows, and the sojourners. Boaz demonstrated his courage and his faith as he boldly, publicly, and selflessly gave Ruth all she needed—far more than her immediate material relief. Boaz gave abundantly from a generous heart.

## A Generous Heart

Why did Boaz show such abundant generosity to a foreign woman? The narrative explains:

> Then she fell on her face, bowing to the ground, and said to him, "Why have I found favor in your eyes, that you should take notice of me, since I am a foreigner?" But Boaz answered her, "All that you have done for your mother-in-law since the death of your husband

has been fully told to me, and how you left your father and mother and your native land and came to a people that you did not know before. The LORD repay you for what you have done, and a full reward be given you by the LORD, the God of Israel, under whose wings you have come to take refuge!" (Ruth 2:8-12)

Boaz knew what Ruth had done for Naomi—how she had given everything to care for her mother-in-law. He understood that it was the Lord who was inviting him to repay Ruth for her generosity and dedication toward Naomi.

Perhaps the most well-known section in the story of Ruth is the scene in which Ruth sought out Boaz in the night. At Naomi's direction, Ruth went to the threshing floor where Boaz was sleeping and tucked herself beneath the corners of his cloak. When he awoke suddenly and saw Ruth at his feet, she said to him: "I am Ruth, your servant. Spread your wings over your servant, for you are a redeemer" (Ruth 3:9a). Ruth's request was that Boaz legally represent the rights of his relatives, namely Naomi and Ruth. Elimelech's land holdings in Bethlehem needed to be redeemed from the debt position in which he had left them ten years before. As redeemer, Boaz had to carefully obey the Law and follow prescribed legal procedures to return ownership to Elimelech's widow and heirs. Agreeing to Ruth's request, Boaz became their redeemer and took on the legal responsibilities. Boaz, driven by a willing heart that extended him beyond the minimal requirements of the Law, took on more than their legal responsibilities; he also took responsibility for continuing the family line and providing an heir for his relative Elimelech.

Therefore, he volunteered to take Ruth to be his wife. Boaz—the esteemed, successful landowner in Bethlehem—united himself to Ruth, the widowed foreign woman from Moab. Boaz gave everything he could to Ruth without regard for his own reputation, the prejudices of his fellow people, or for his own economic investment in the redemption process. He pledged and gave to Ruth his entire life. That generosity and sacrificial, selfless giving is a reflection of the God whom Boaz served and obeyed.

Boaz's generosity and abundant giving, revealing his willing heart and God-directed spirit, manifested itself in three ways: through his provision, through his protection, and through his promise.

## Provision

Not only did Boaz give Ruth permission to glean in his field but he also counseled her *not* to glean in any fields belonging to other men. Ruth could rely on Boaz to provide her with all her material needs. By giving her provision, he showed he cared for her. Going even further, Boaz gave Ruth a preferred portion of the provision. He instructed his foremen to deliberately drop full bundles of the harvested grain in Ruth's path as she gleaned, making sure she had more than enough. "And also pull out some from the bundles for her and leave it for her to glean. And do not rebuke her" (Ruth 2:16). Lastly and most intimately, Boaz boldly gave Ruth, a foreigner of a pagan people, a place of privilege at his lunch table and shared his drink and food with her.

## Protection

Boaz's giving to Ruth included a guarantee of protection. He offered her a hedge of protection while she worked during the harvest by instructing his foremen and the reapers to keep Ruth safe from any harassment that might be directed to a young single woman alone in a strange land. Ruth recognized Boaz's generous heart through his generosity. When Ruth slipped into his resting place on the threshing floor and covered herself with the wings of his cloak, she was ultimately asking for his formal, legal protection under the Law. In the immediate awkward situation of a close encounter between unmarried people, Boaz protected her reputation by ensuring her privacy. He went further by protecting her future reputation, agreeing to act as kinsman redeemer. Boaz knew that redemption would include taking Ruth in marriage and grafting her into the community of God's people.

## Promise

Boaz gave Ruth a promise. He affirmed that he would act as kinsman to redeem Naomi's property and, in the process, take custody of Ruth. Boaz held true to his promise and redeemed the property for Naomi—and ultimately married Ruth. The promise was to be not just redeemer but head of the family she had lost. The Lord blessed Boaz's and Ruth's faith and gave them a son. Boaz's promise extended beyond Ruth and covered Naomi as well. The women of Bethlehem rejoiced at the birth of Obed and declared, "The Lord has given Naomi a son" (Ruth 4:17). Boaz models for us the true spirit of giving. He was obedient to the Law, the Word of God, by providing Ruth the material provision laid out in the Law. He demonstrated the greater spirit of the Law by giving generously and sacrificially out of a willing heart and a generous spirit. Through Boaz's giving spirit, the Lord provided Ruth with all she could have asked for. These blessings all came from God's providential hand.

## A Legacy of Giving and Grace

One important biblical principle of giving is that by God's transformative power, giving blesses individuals, families, *and* communities. We have seen so far how Boaz gave Ruth his provision (grain and food for sustenance), his protection (desperately needed by a foreign widow in a strange land), and his promise (to redeem Naomi's land and take Ruth for a wife). The generous giving of Boaz—which went beyond his obligations under the Law toward the poor, the sojourner, and the widow—blessed others in myriad ways that Boaz could not have anticipated or foreseen.

Boaz blessed Ruth, who, a stranger in a strange land, received a new life as a daughter of Israel, as a wife and as a mother. Boaz himself was blessed as he received a faithful, honorable woman for a wife and a son as his heir. Naomi and her deceased husband (Elimelech) and sons (Mahlon and Chilion) were blessed by the redemption of the family property and the continuation of the family line through Obed. The community of Bethlehem was blessed as they rejoiced over the gift of God to Naomi—her restoration from her brokenness and the blessing of an heir. The women of Bethlehem demonstrated their connection to the child by giving him his name: "And the women of the neighborhood gave him a name, saying, 'A son has been born to Naomi.' They named him Obed. He was the father of Jesse, the father of David" (Ruth 4:17). This is the only instance in the Old Testament where a child is named by anyone other than the parents or by God. The community of Israel was also blessed to see a baby born who would be in the line of the promised Messiah, Jesus. And we today are blessed that God supplied Boaz with a heart willing to give—that God used Boaz and Ruth in his plan of redemption to continue the Messianic line through their son, Obed. This is grandiose giving. By God's sovereign plan, even you and I today are blessed because of Boaz.

One evening, I returned home from work to find my wife, Heather, on her way to her friend Janelle's house. Heather explained that Janelle's daughter, Sarah, would soon be departing for an overseas mission trip with a group of fellow students. Heather and a group were going to pray over Sarah that night. Heather invited me to come along, but I declined. But as I listened to her, I suddenly remembered I had a hundred-dollar bill in my wallet. It had been there a long time, a remainder from a garage sale. There's not much use these days for a hundred-dollar bill, so I had just stuck it in my wallet. Without too much thought, I took the bill from my wallet and gave it to my wife, who put it in a card as a gift for seventeen-year-old Sarah. I had no idea how much impact that hundred-dollar bill would have.

The next day, Heather told me an incredible story. As Sarah's parents were driving her from Colorado Springs to the Denver International Airport, Sarah suddenly realized that she had forgotten her hiking boots. Given the type of work Sarah would be doing in Zambia, she knew she was going to need a good pair of boots. So, her parents stopped at an outlet mall on the interstate, and Sarah found new boots for $40 without too much hassle. They got back into the car and continued on to the airport.

Her parents dropped her off, said good-bye, and left Sarah. Upon arriving at the airline check-in desk, Sarah quickly ran into another dilemma: because she was only seventeen, the international airline would not allow her to board the plane and fly to Africa without a signed and notarized form of parental consent. Sarah was the only student in her class under eighteen. Her parents were on the road back to Colorado Springs when Sarah called and told them they had to turn around so they could come and sign the permission form. They agreed and came speeding back—only to realize the form had to be notarized, and of course, there was no notary in the Denver International Airport. Miraculously, Sarah and the airline personnel were able to locate a mobile notary that came to the airport just in time to notarize the parental consent form and get Sarah on the plane in the nick of time. The notary cost $60.

Between her boots and the notary fee, Sarah unexpectedly spent exactly $100 to get on the flight and begin her mission trip. When I heard this story, I knew exactly why God had sealed that hundred-dollar bill in my wallet for all those weeks. He knew that one night he would use me to provide for Sarah's needs so she could minister to the hurting people of Zambia. The impact of my giving was greater than I could have known. I really didn't have any idea that my gift would be used by God to bless so many others. What's more, in his sovereignty, God orchestrated these events to remind us that he always provides for his children. And he often invites us to join in as his agents of mercy and giving. This is what I call the "Boaz effect" of giving—when our giving blesses those far beyond the recipient of the gift, and far beyond what we can foresee. From this story and from the story of Boaz, I hope you begin to see the far-reaching impact that the Lord can make through our acts of giving. Like Boaz, may we learn to give beyond what's required as we give to those in need, and trust in God's sovereignty to use us to share his blessings far beyond what we will ever see or what we could ever imagine.

## *For Further Reflection*

1. What about this story most resonated with you? How can it be applied in your own or your community's life?
2. How would you describe Ruth's character and generosity?
3. How would you describe Boaz's character and generosity?
4. What legacy and ripple effect did Boaz's giving beyond the Law have on the people of Israel? In the church today?
5. Where are you being called to give beyond the Law?

# PART THREE
# GIVING FOSTERS COMMUNITY

# CHAPTER SIX

# GIVING IN DISAPPOINTMENT

In the final portion of this book, I want to explore how giving fosters community. Boaz, as we have already seen, is a supreme example of how giving can have long-lasting, unforeseen impact on God's people. But we have not yet plumbed the depths of all the Old Testament has to say about giving. Now we turn to another famous figure, Boaz and Ruth's great-grandson, King David. David's story of giving is distinct from that of Boaz. While Boaz gave from abundance and a prospect of a brighter future for himself, David gave in disappointment—when his personal plans were subsumed by God's greater plan for all of Israel.

## The King's Desire

David's lifelong dream was to build a house for the Lord. In Psalm 24 he wrote that he desired to "dwell in the house of the Lord forever." He desired to create a place where God's presence would dwell with his people permanently. David had lived his whole life in service to the Lord and in expectation of the day when he would be able to take down the portable tabernacle and build a permanent house for the ark of the covenant. As king, David had the authority and the resources to build such a temple. But the Lord had different plans.

Now, it is important to recount David's track record at this point. David was called a "man after God's own heart"—and for good reason! But David's life was also marked by a disastrous sin, as seen in the well-known story of David's fall into adultery with Bathsheba and the murder of her husband, David's loyal soldier:

> It happened, late one afternoon, when David arose from his couch and was walking on the roof of the king's house, that he saw from the roof a woman bathing; and the woman was very beautiful. And David sent and inquired about the woman. And one said, "Is not this Bathsheba, the daughter of Eliam, the wife of Uriah the Hittite?" So David sent messengers and took her, and she came to him, and he lay with her. (Now she had been purifying herself from her uncleanness.) Then she returned to her house. And the woman conceived, and she sent and told David, "I am pregnant." (2 Sam 11:2-5)

The story only gets worse from here. David knew Bathsheba's husband was out at war, fighting for Israel. Thus David sent a letter to his commanding officer, Joab, to have Uriah killed. "In the letter he wrote, 'Set Uriah in the forefront of the hardest fighting, and then draw back from him, that he may be struck down, and die'" (2 Sam 11:15). Joab obeyed David's malicious order, abandoning Uriah in the heat of battle—leaving him alone to be slaughtered by the enemies. And thus "the man after God's own heart" orchestrated adultery and murder in one fell swoop.

On the one hand, David's sin reminds us of wicked King Ahab and Jezebel. Both kings coveted what was not theirs to have (Ahab a neighbor's vineyard, David a married woman). And both of these kings murdered valiant, honorable men to take possession of their heart's desire. On the other hand, David's story deviates from Ahab's because he eventually repented of his sin and turned to God. Psalm 51 reveals David's change of heart: "Have mercy on me, O God, according to your steadfast love; according to your abundant mercy blot out my transgressions. Wash me thoroughly from my iniquity, and cleanse me from my sin!" (Ps 51:1-2). This is why David, and not Ahab, is remembered as a man after God's own heart. David acknowledged his iniquity and turned to the Lord for forgiveness. In his mercy, God forgave David for his sin. But he did not spare him from punishment that came as a result of all the consequences of his choices. One form of punishment was his disqualification from being the builder of the Lord's temple. Ultimately, we see evidence of David's true repentance through his generous giving.

## The Great Disappointment

Years later, the time has finally come to build the temple; David's dream was about to become reality. When the season came for breaking ground, the Lord informed David that he was not worthy to lead the project, as there was too much blood on his hands. Instead, David's son, Solomon, would be the one to build the temple in Jerusalem. How did David react to this bad news? We might expect him to be disappointed, to question his faith, or even to actively subvert the project if he couldn't have his way. On the contrary, we see a positive reaction from David, expressed through his generous giving. David's joyful, faithful response stands in stark contrast to Cain's bitter reaction to disappointment as we recounted in chapter 1. When God rejected Cain's offering, his face fell and he turned from God and grew angry. We might have expected David to react in like fashion when God told him he could not lead the temple project. Instead, David adjusted, submitted to God's authority, and sought alternative ways that he could participate in God's building plan.

David learned an important lesson. Just because *our* plans are thwarted does not mean that God's plans are. And when God says no, it may not mean rejection, but redirection. As we seek to obey God's will, David's realization should encourage us: God is always sovereign over and intimately connected with our circumstances and desires. His plans do not fail. David acknowledged that God had short-circuited his dream of leading the temple construction, but he did not give up entirely; rather, he found a new role to play in the endeavor. Even in his disappointment, David chose to join the community and give. When we give our time, talents, and treasures as we are able, we consecrate ourselves to the Lord's purposes. Giving is often the means by which we participate in God's plan and serve his purposes. Are you confessing through your giving that you submit to God's plan and are willingly joined to his purposes?

David's decision to press on in the face of disappointment was not a private affair. He turned to the public assembly and told them that God had denied him the privilege of building the temple. That public confession could not have been an easy task. In spite of his rejection, David offered his full support to the project by giving from the royal treasury and, on top of that, his entire personal fortune—all his gold, silver, and precious possessions. He engaged in the community's project to honor the Lord with a humble, willing servant's heart. In response, the leaders of Israel heard David's generous, self-sacrificing pledge and responded in faith and in action, giving from their own personal wealth. By his dramatic, passionate, and joyful act of giving, David inspired his community to follow him and likewise give generously, joyfully, and fearlessly.

## The Great Participation

David gave through a magnificent public gift. In many churches today, Christians are timid about giving in view of others. They fear appearing haughty or legalistic. So they remain content placing their anonymous envelope in the offering basket each Sunday. David, however, offered his resources for the temple in the sight of all Israel without feeling bashful. Rather, through his public display of generosity toward the Lord's work, he engaged, inspired, and invited the community to join in what God was doing through Solomon. In a sense, David exhorted everyone to be generous givers and made the lead gift—a gift that would spark a communal fire of giving for God's plans. "Then the people rejoiced because they had given willingly, for with a whole heart they had offered freely to the LORD. David the king also rejoiced greatly" (1 Chr 29:9).

Giving in community can be a contagious practice. Sometimes all it takes for our hearts to be rekindled to give is the sight of a friend making sacrifices or directing offerings to God's work. And conversely, we must understand that our public giving (particularly before the eyes of the church) has the power to catalyze others. When we share in giving *to* and *with* one another, we unite ourselves to God's Kingdom and identity with *his* ways. As we have discussed, such selfless giving is the fruit of hearts who understand that God owns everything—our time, our money, and our being. Pause for a moment and review this chapter as an opportunity to assess the giving patterns and rhythms of the Christian community to which you belong. Does your community inspire you by the way they give? If not, what steps can you take to elicit joy in others? How can you help transform the standards and patterns of giving in your community through the way *you* give to the Lord?

King David teaches us a number of important lessons about giving in disappointment. First, giving is not just our appropriate response when God blesses us. David's generosity came on the heels of bad news from the Lord. Through his giving, David evidenced a positive outward expression of faith and love for the Lord, even when his own plans and dreams went unfulfilled. Second, we learn that God owns it all. Giving to the temple all that he had was David's duty as a good and faithful steward of his God-given wealth. And third, David's giving was not merely a private transaction between him and the Lord. It was an individual act loudly expressed as part of a community of faith. He gave publicly to be an inspiration to the entire nation. In the end, David's royal leadership took the form not of the construction management role he craved but that of a fundraising leader.

## A Lead Gift Without Any Money

One day we at WaterStone received a phone call from an excited Nebraskan woman named Sheila. She explained her predicament to

me: "I've just been named chairman of my church building committee. I know I am expected to give a lead gift to the building project,
but I have no money. What do I do?" We quickly learned that Sheila
and her husband, Ben, owned and operated a farm in Nebraska.
While Ben did most of the farming, Sheila managed the business
dimension. And what she told us was true: they had no money to
give. While this was not a promising start to a conversation about
giving, we were impressed by their determination to find a way.
Sheila and Ben had no money, but they had something much more
valuable—*willing hearts.*

As productive farmers, this couple could count on an annual
abundant harvest. As we assessed their giving potential, we told
Sheila this good news: "If you don't have any money, bring your
harvest instead. Rather than selling all of your corn and soybeans
at the grain elevator, gift a portion of the crop to an account that
WaterStone will open. The value of this gift to your WaterStone
Giving Fund will not be included in your federal, income, or self-
employment taxes—potentially saving you more than fifty percent
in taxes you'd send to Uncle Sam. You can then advise WaterStone
to direct the funds from your WaterStone Giving Fund to your
church building fund." How did Sheila and Ben respond to our
idea? They opened a WaterStone Giving Fund and deposited one
hundred thousand dollars' worth of their harvest into it. Over time,
most of the money generated from the gift of grain went directly to
their church and to the causes they supported. For a couple with no
money to give to their church, they were able to present a lead gift
of one hundred thousand dollars. Since then, Sheila and Ben have
donated annually from their harvests, and through their WaterStone

Giving Fund, they've been blessed to make over six hundred thousand dollars in charitable gifts to their church and other nonprofits about which they are passionate.

Sheila's church building committee used the money from their donation to build a new church school in their town. Their gift gave the gift of a Christian education to children, but the impact of their giving didn't stop there. Like Sheila, many of the members in her church were also farmers with little cash available to give. When they *saw* her and her husband give such an abundant lead gift toward the church building project committee, they began to ask: *Where did you find that kind of money? How were you able to give like that?* Thus, through her gift, Sheila was able to share the giving strategy that had saved her on taxes and given her cash to give. Sheila's heart for giving resulted in more than one large gift. It inspired and equipped farmers to steward their own agricultural resources and use them as a source for giving, blessing the community, and joining them together in God's mission.

Today, the work of the Lord continues through churches, ministries, and charities. From the story of David we can draw strength to give generously. Through giving, we express our faith and trust in the Lord. Through giving, we honor God. Through giving, we can inspire others to join together in a more generous community of shared faith and commitment to the Lord. Then, even in times of disappointment, we can declare with David:

> Therefore David blessed the LORD in the presence of all the assembly. And David said: "Blessed are you, O LORD, the God of Israel our father, forever and ever. Yours, O LORD, is the greatness

and the power and the glory and the victory and the majesty, for all that is in the heavens and in the earth is yours. Yours is the kingdom, O LORD, and you are exalted as head above all. Both riches and honor come from you, and you rule over all. In your hand are power and might, and in your hand it is to make great and to give strength to all. And now we thank you, our God, and praise your glorious name." (1 Chr 29:10-13)

## *For Further Reflection*

1. What about this story of David and the temple most resonated with you? How can the example of the temple project be applied in your own or your community's life?

2. Put yourself in David's sandals. Would your heart still be willing to serve—and even give abundantly—if your personal plan for a church or ministry project was vetoed?

3. What are the standards for giving in your Christian community? Are they challenging, exciting, and fearless? Or are they comfortable, passive, and timid?

4. How do you feel about David's public, lead gift toward the temple project? What was the benefit of his pledging his support so vocally and openly?

5. Is there an action you can take—a generous gift, a commitment to serve as a volunteer or church leader—that God is calling you to commit to and declare publicly to inspire others?

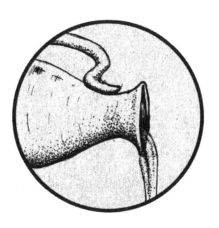

# CHAPTER SEVEN

# DROPS OF OIL

## The Widow's Crisis

There once lived a woman in a village of Israel. This woman's husband—the son of a prophet—had recently passed away, leaving her with mountains of debt and two young sons who were too young to care for her. Adding to the dilemma, her family's creditors had come to collect—and had threatened to take the widow's two sons to be slaves in lieu of payment. She had no money to pay back her husband's debts, and the weight of social stigma was a heavy burden. The woman knew she had only one hope in this situation—God himself. So she turned for help to Elisha, a prophet and a man of God.

As a prophet, Elisha spoke on behalf of God to his people. The Bible tells us that Elisha was at heart a servant, called by the Lord from his life as a prosperous farmer to serve Elijah and all Israel. In fact, kings came to Elisha for his wisdom and sage advice (2 Kgs 3:11). Thus, when this widow recognized that only God could deliver her family from this crisis, she turned to Elisha—a man who spoke for God and to God on behalf of his people. Sometimes God sends his help through people, and many times God transmits his will for us in the form of people of faith. As we will see, God used ordinary folks to provide wisdom, direction, and protection for the widow and her sons. It's worth noting that many times God's help comes to us in disguise. Hear the dialogue between the widow and Elisha:

> And Elisha said to her, "What shall I do for you? Tell me; what have you in the house?" And she said, "Your servant has nothing in the house except a jar of oil." Then he said, "Go outside, borrow vessels from all your neighbors, empty vessels and not too few. Then go in and shut the door behind yourself and your sons and pour into all these vessels. And when one is full, set it aside." So she went from him and shut the door behind herself and her sons. And as she poured they brought the vessels to her. When the vessels were full, she said to her son, "Bring me another vessel." And he said to her, "There is not another." Then the oil stopped flowing. She came and told the man of God, and he said, "Go, sell the oil and pay your debts, and you and your sons can live on the rest." (2 Kgs 4:2-7)

What is even more striking than this woman's difficult situation is her source for her solution: in faith she chose to run to God first. As the wife of a prophet in dark times in Israel, she was part of a tradition of faith and a member of God's people—his remnant. However, her faith did not prevent her time of troubles and did not immediately alleviate the impending doom to her household. Like Noah, the widow expressed her faith in God by putting him first. She didn't go to her neighbors for financial assistance. She didn't go to the king or governing authorities for a legal opinion. She turned to the man of God because she knew intuitively that God would provide for her—even in her pit of trouble. In acute crisis, her focus, hope, and heart were in the right place—focused on the Lord.

## What's in Your Cupboard?

Elisha's role as advisor in this story reveals God's providential hand. God works to help his people who are in need through the agency of his ministers and servants. Elisha was able to see the bigger picture of God's providence in this drama—he not only properly assessed the widow's needs but also recognized that God, who had sent Elisha to this widow, was already at work behind the scenes to deliver this widow and at the same time refine her faith. This testing of the widow's faith was evident through Elisha's question: "What do you have in your house?" Elisha invited the widow to be a part of her own solution. God was the source of the deliverance, but she had a part to play. And not just her, but her sons and her neighbors. Though she did not yet know it, God had already provided the seeds of salvation from her pressing needs. Thus, she wasn't merely a woman without any answers; God had equipped her with a solution of which she was completely unaware: a few drops of oil.

Seasons of financial want can be stifling for anyone. Unexpected bills, the loss of a job, and health emergencies all may disrupt our economic balance and peace. Giving may be the last thing on our minds when money is tight and we're struggling to merely make ends meet. The burden is not just economic; it can be spiritual. This story speaks to us when we pass through those waters of hard times because it reminds us that God has always met and will always meet our needs. The widow's oil represents our reservoir of faith in times of our darkest troubles. God promises to recognize our faith, use it for his glory, and multiply it for our benefit. Jesus tells us even faith like a grain of mustard seed can move mountains (Matt 17:20). The widow might not have seen God's provision before connecting with Elisha, but she did have the faith to run to God first—refusing to take matters into her own hands, turn to the world for its solutions, and thereby turn *from* her trust in God and turn *to* unbelief.

## Jars, Jars, and More Jars

Once Elisha made the widow aware of her God-given resources, her few drops of oil, Elisha related his plan. His solution to the widow's problem was as profound and as simple as his initial question. He commanded her to go into her neighborhood and borrow empty jars, "and not too few." The woman complied and sent her sons to gather vessels from the surrounding community. Consequently, both boys became active agents in the solution to their dilemma alongside their mother. But the invitation to join in the solution to the widow's problem didn't stop there. As they walked from door to door, the sons also invited the community into God's providential rescue plan: by asking to borrow vessels, the sons were inviting the neighbors to participate in God's saving work and to express their own faith by giving. The neighbors gave their jars willingly. Perhaps they were relieved that the sons hadn't come to ask for money to pay off the debt. Money? No way. Jars? No problem. Each gave what they could (at least in terms of jars) with a willing heart. By God's design, the solution was in community, not isolation. And the problem was not just the widow's debt; it was the neighbors' lack of generosity and compassion in not helping the widow voluntarily.

It is worth noting that *no one* in this story was required by God to give money. What God required from the sons and from the community was faith and jars—not financial sacrifice. The neighbors were likely more willing to give because God required only a token gift. He did not require much, yet he offered them an opportunity to give and bless a woman in need. We must realize that we do not *need* to have or give money to play a role in God's Kingdom work. Since God has already provided everything we need to conquer hard times, what we need to give is unquestioning faith and obedience.

Once the sons had collected a surplus of vessels, they returned home and, with their mother, began to fill them with oil. Behind a closed door, she began to pour from the "jar of a few drops" and filled up every vessel that her sons had gathered until there were no more. Her single, sparsely filled jar miraculously overflowed into numerous vessels of oil—"and not too few." As soon as they ran out of vessels, the flow of oil ceased. God matched the generosity of the community to the drop. When they had no more vessels to give, he had no more oil to give. Elisha then commanded her, "Go, sell the oil and pay your debts, and you and your sons can live on the rest" (2 Kgs 4:7). Can you imagine the wonder that must have overtaken the woman? She went from having "nothing in the house except a jar of oil" to a house overflowing with oil-filled jars. God not only provided as much as she needed to relieve her from debt but also provided for her and her family indefinitely. This was a work of God's superabundant provision.

## Superabundant Provision

God is the center of every story in the Bible. His providential hand is especially evident in stories like this one. Through Elisha, God both tested and cared for a desperate widow and her sons, engaging them in order to multiply their trust in him. According to his divine purpose, God invited the community to participate in *his* giving. Lastly, he delivered the widow from her calamitous situation and superabundantly provided for her. God's work through Elisha reminds us of Boaz's provision for Ruth. Boaz gave above and beyond what anyone expected of him, and his actions rippled through his community and across time. Similarly, God used a few drops of oil to redeem the widow and her sons. When the community saw God's provision, they must have been chastened, humbled, and blessed that God had stepped in to help while they had not. Through the widow's circumstances, God was simultaneously testing and blessing the community.

God continues to test his people today. He calls us, as individuals and communities, to emulate the faith of the widow from this story. When God tested her through trials, she turned for help to the Lord. By turning to Elisha, she acknowledged that God's provision is often channeled through our brothers and sisters. In the same way, God challenges us to step up, help his people, our brothers and sisters, by being superabundant givers. Has the Lord placed a person in need in your path? Is he inviting you to lend a jar to a neighbor in need? God's Word tells us that God tests us to refine us into a people who are more like Christ. We must be open to the opportunities for giving that God places before us, and we must, in faith, answer the call and respond by giving—giving whatever we can provide.

When we give to others, we are giving to God. God does not *need* anything from us, but he does desire our fellowship and our worship. Giving, moreover, is a transformational facet of worship. Jesus told his disciples that their actions toward people in need equated with their actions toward him. "Truly, I say to you, as you did it to one of the least of these my brothers, you did it to me" (Matt 25:40). On the one hand, this is a frightening claim. When we engage with people in our daily lives, we can truly say that we encounter Jesus *every day*. When we ignore the needs of those around us, we ignore Jesus. On the other hand, Jesus's words remind us that he gives us ample, real-world opportunities to express our faith through giving.

When you truly love someone, you *joyfully* seek out what pleases and honors them and makes them happy—and you do it. God as Trinity is a relationship of one God in three persons united in selfless love. God designed men in his image to reflect this dynamic of selfless love. But how can we know what God loves? What pleases and honors him? The answer is in God's Word. In John 14:15, Jesus says, "If you love me, you will keep my commandments." And conversely, "Whoever does not love me does not keep my words" (John 14:24a). Our challenge is to discover how to obey Jesus's commandments and keep his words. Giving provides one way we can respond to Jesus.

In all of our giving, we can only give back to God what is already his. It all belongs to God. Whether we see it or not, God has super-abundantly provided us with everything we need to keep his words. In John 15:12-13 Jesus lays out his expectation for his followers plainly: "This is my commandment, that you love one another as I have loved you. Greater love has no one than this, that someone lay down his life for his friends." Through giving, we are able to display our love for God and our love for our neighbors. Through sacrificial giving we can lay down our lives—our time, treasures, and talents—for our friends *and* enemies. Jesus laid down his life for us through a sacrificial gift. He gave everything. Now, Jesus expects us to be his agents of transformation in the world. We are to feed his sheep with the gospel, care for widows and orphans, feed the hungry, and comfort the afflicted. In faith we give and sacrifice to honor God and minister to his people. We love because he first loved us.

When God comes first, structuring our lives is easier. The widow's life was clearly not easy—but her faith in God carried her through trouble. From this story we learn two lessons. First, our acts of giving, through God's providence, bless us. God uses our giving to bless not just the direct beneficiaries of the gifts but also the givers, agents, advisors, and all those who are witnesses to the transformational power of giving. Second, God extends to us a promise: "Give me everything you have. I will give you everything you need." Giving expresses faith that God can and does provide for his people super-abundantly. Our faithful trust must stand even as we commit our manifold resources that seem absolutely vital to our livelihood. God's plans, purposes, and Kingdom will prevail in the end. Giving is one way we can conform our simple lives to his plans. When we faithfully entwine God's pattern for giving into our lives, we can be certain he is transforming us more closely to his image. So what's in your cupboard? How has God already prepared you to go and give? "For we are his workmanship, created in Christ Jesus for good works, which God prepared beforehand, that we should walk in them" (Eph 2:10).

## *For Further Reflection*

1. What in this story of the widow's oil most resonated with you? How can it be applied to your own life or your faith community's life?
2. When you are in need, do you run to man-made solutions, or to the Lord first?
3. Are you being called to lend a simple "jar" to someone in need? If yes, is there more you *could* be doing to help? What's stopping you from acting today?
4. Do you joyfully seek out through giving what pleases and honors God?
5. Do you diligently love "the least of these" as if you're loving Jesus himself?

# CONCLUSION

As we have seen in these stories, God invites his people into his plans, and giving is one way we can participate in those plans. The Old Testament is laden with both figures who modeled heart-level, selfless giving and figures who modeled selfish idolatry. When God invites us to give, he gives us the opportunity to trust in his provision for our lives and to worship him in thanksgiving for that provision. God has already given us all we need to give.

The earthly ministry of Jesus was the ultimate invitation to men to give. Jesus did not own anything, yet he spent his life blessing, healing, and ultimately saving the sick, poor, and needy. Jesus borrowed a manger in which to be born. Jesus had to borrow a fishing boat to preach from so that he could give words of life to others. Jesus borrowed a few loaves and fish from a lad to feed the hungry multitudes. Jesus had to borrow a colt when he entered Jerusalem for the last time. When it came time for the Last Supper, Jesus commanded his disciples to borrow an upper room for them to dine in. After he was crucified, Jesus had to borrow a tomb in which he could be buried. At every phase of his ministry, Jesus invited others to join with him through giving.

As Christians today, we cannot give into the earthly life of Jesus, but we can give into the lives of the faithful and the lives of those who do not know him. Each of us must examine our own heart with humility and honesty before the Lord. Do we give generously? Is God the first thing in our lives? As we learn to give with joyful hearts, we become the hands and feet of Jesus on this earth. This is what it means to participate in God's plans and purposes for all people. When we give with open arms and generous hearts, we help build God's Kingdom on this earth. Jesus began his ministry by declaring his messianic purpose. Reading from the words of the prophet Isaiah, Jesus said:

> The Spirit of the Lord GOD is upon me, because the LORD has anointed me to bring good news to the poor; he has sent me to bind up the brokenhearted, to proclaim liberty to the captives, and the opening of the prison to those who are bound; to proclaim the year of the LORD's favor, and the day of vengeance of our God; to comfort all who mourn; to grant to those who mourn in Zion—to give them a beautiful headdress instead of ashes, the oil of gladness instead of mourning, the garment of praise instead of a faint spirit; that they may be called oaks of righteousness, the planting of the LORD, that he may be glorified. (Isa 61:1-3)

I pray this book has allowed you to remember all that God has done for you. He has given you everything you need to give. Now, in faith, may we accept his invitation to live with radical generosity in a selfish world. May our giving be worshipful, nuanced, heartfelt expressions of love for our neighbor and faith in God. When we give, what's most important is not the size of the gift but the size of the heart behind the gift. When we give, we are to open our hearts and let the Spirt of God shape our decisions and our actions. When we put first things first, we are freed to give generously, sacrificially, joyfully, and fearlessly.

# ABOUT THE AUTHOR

As Vice President of Giving Strategies, Will's mission is to connect Christian givers, professional advisors, and nonprofit leaders to the innovative giving solutions, services, and educational resources that WaterStone offers. WaterStone is a financial ministry, a Christian public foundation and 501(c)(3), providing innovative giving strategies to givers in order to multiply the resources they make available to ministries for the building of the Kingdom. In this capacity Will is blessed to meet church and ministry leaders, and brothers and sisters in Christ around the world and connect them to one another in a community of giving.

Will spent twenty years on Wall Street as a sales and marketing executive, first as senior vice president at Morgan Stanley Investment Management, and then as chief marketing officer at 1st Global Capital. Will began his professional career as a high school English teacher and head football coach at Brooklyn's Tilden High School, where his Blue Devil teams won back-to-back New York City division championships.

In 2009, the Lord called Will out of the business world and led him to Southwestern Baptist Theological Seminary, where he earned his Master of Divinity in Biblical Languages and Steward Leadership. He is currently working toward his PhD with a focus on an Old Testament theology of giving. Will is an ordained minister of God's Word and is blessed to be invited to preach and teach throughout the country. Will and his wife, Heather, live in Colorado Springs. Their family includes three sons, a grandmother, two cats, two cockatiels, and a wicked-smart rescue dog who faithfully protects the family as his chosen pack members.

Will is available to preach, speak, or teach about giving and the gospel and its application to God-honoring fundraising. Contact Will to invite him to present at your church, professional conference, ministry meeting, or classroom.

## Contact and Speaking

**Email:**     polyprep1975@outlook.com
**Phone:**    (719) 447-4620
**LinkedIn:**  linkedin.com/in/williamjohnstevens

# ABOUT WATERSTONE

Honoring God. Serving Givers. Building the Kingdom.

Honoring God. Serving Givers. Building the Kingdom.
WaterStone is a Christian public foundation 501(c)(3) that exists to honor God, serve givers, and build the Kingdom. We come alongside givers, advisors and ministries to provide trusted counsel and tax-smart innovative giving strategies. Our expertise is working with business owners and stewards of family wealth to unlock the giving potential of their non-cash assets like real estate, business interests, oil/gas, and agricultural commodities. With WaterStone, you work with experienced Christian business leaders who are aligned with your core values and share your biblical worldview. WaterStone is blessed to be called by the Lord to be part of his Kingdom-building project. WaterStone is all about giving. We strive to empower the building of the Kingdom by providing expertise to the Christian community on how to give intentionally. At the heart of our mission, we educate and equip givers to help steer vital financial

support to the churches, ministries, and charities that do the Lord's work every day.

We help families create a legacy of giving. In that legacy is the conviction that we are called to be good and faithful stewards of all that the Lord entrusts to us. Through WaterStone, families can multiply their giving impact for the Kingdom, minimize taxes, and heighten their joy of generosity.

## Contact WaterStone

| | |
|---|---|
| **Website:** | WaterStone.org |
| **Email:** | info@waterstone.org |
| **Phone:** | (719) 447-4620 |
| **Fax:** | (719) 447-4700 |
| **Address:** | WaterStone |
| | 10807 New Allegiance Drive, Suite 240 |
| | Colorado Springs, CO 80921 |
| **Facebook:** | Facebook.com/WaterStoneOrg |
| **Twitter:** | Twitter.com/WaterStoneOrg |
| **LinkedIn:** | LinkedIn.com/company/waterstone |